Dedication

I want to dedicate my first book to all of the fallen angels out there

Who I know will become discovered angels

With time, support, and resilience………

To my sisters, Shantai and Jessica

Who have been by my side through everything

To Michael H., who encouraged me to keep pushing for what I wanted

And who never hesitated to answer any questions I had.

And to Randi H. and Eric Q.,

Who were very helpful and patient with me during production.

Table of Contents

To the Readers

This book can be difficult to read. It may even be mentally exhausting especially if you feel you're in a terrible place. Some of the stories may sound like your own and take you back to a memory that you hate. But in order to get better, we have to go down that path. We have to clean all of the dirty cobwebs out of the closet.

If you feel like this book is becoming overwhelming, immediately put the book down. Pick it up when you have more strength. Read it in a safe place, in a safe surrounding where there is a shoulder if you need it. But do me a favor, make it through the book.

I can guarantee you I have been in your position, close to it, or worse off. But the more I talk about my issues, the less they weigh heavily on me. The less they control my thoughts and my dreams. The less power they have. If you read something that hits home, talk about it with someone you trust. Get it off your chest. Or simply just write it down. Use this book to relate and analyze your personal situation.

I know this; women are built very strong. You can and will make it through your struggles. If no one else believes in you, know that I do. You're thinking: "she doesn't even know me". You're right. I don't know you personally. But as I said, women are built strong, very strong! So pat your hair, adjust that bra, and let's do this!

Prologue

One day I just woke up and the world was crashing down before my eyes. My past trailed behind me like a rattlesnake. Ready to poison me repeatedly as it had done so many times. I realized that the air I was breathing was suffocating me.

I needed a new environment. I needed to breathe. But I had been in this place for so long, I didn't know how to get out. I couldn't even afford a road map, let alone a GPS.

Everyone had deserted me. Or maybe I had deserted them first. Every day I wanted to cry out for my mommy, my daddy. But my voice was hoarse from all this screaming in my head. I was raised on fairy tales, pretty dresses, and the promise of a handsome prince. I fell on empty dreams, broken promises, and guilt.

I dug a hole so deep, the only way for someone to find me was to fall in with me. But I continued tunneling. I tunneled through the dirt, the grime, trying to find a light. Climbed out when I could; fell in again when I wasn't looking. When my mind and body said I had had enough.

But then I met them; the fallen angels. Women who used to dream like me. Women who felt the things I felt, who fell into the same hole. I hated them. Because they were a reflection of who I was. And I hated my reflection.

But they begin to talk, so did I. We understood one another. I had found them, these fallen angels, and somehow, someone also found us.

Chapter 1

Fallen Angels

Cheyenne

My life was falling apart. Those I worked with begin losing respect for me. Family was hearing from me less and less. Friends no longer wanted to hang out with me, nor I with them.

My social network was dwindling fast but I didn't notice until the morning I stood tall in front of my superior. His image became blurry as hot wet tears rolled down my face. Because of my actions, I would permanently have a mark on my record for bad conduct. The first mark on my record after 5 years in service.

My superior sent me out of his office to fix myself. Most men didn't like tears no matter what the circumstances. I can only imagine how poorly I looked. I had that hangover look. Tears spilling over and hair disheveled because I put no effort into getting dressed this morning. I walked out of his office, avoiding the eyes of those I worked with. I knew rumors floated around fast. I let the rest of my tears out and reported back in.

My superior read the police report. He read my misconduct. He told me how badly my actions reflected on the unit, how I looked as a leader. He told me the consequences if this were to happen again. I agreed and formally signed the document stating what he discussed.

All he said had been true. My actions last night were that of a child having a fit. My superior directed me to report to the substance abuse counselor in the next 30 minutes. I properly acknowledged him and I left.

****

I signed in at the front desk. It was mandated that I take a breathalyzer. I'd never taken one before. I felt criminal as I blew. Thankfully, I blew low. I drank so much the night before, however, that the alcohol still registered in my system. Not to mention when they released me from the hospital for suicidal thoughts, I went back to my room and drank until I slept.

The counselor took all of the normal information; my name, my unit, my age, why I was referred here. He then went over my family history; were there other alcoholics or drug abusers? Anyone depressed? How much do I normally drink and how often?

At the end of his line of questioning, I was stunned to hear him say I was classified as an alcoholic. I would be sent to rehabilitation for 30 days with those who abused or were addicted to alcohol and drugs. Some military, some not. I would leave for rehab within a week.

I walked out to the parking lot, started my car, and lit a cigarette. My mind was racing. What had I done? Would this hurt the rest of my career? Could I ever mentally bounce back from this?

I laid my head down on the steering wheel and cried the little tears I had left. I didn't know whether I was heading up or down, left or right. But I was headed somewhere. In this cycle, I had lived for two years. Honestly, I needed the break.

Jennifer

I held my head down as the judge spoke about her disappointment in the youth today. She sounded like my father used to. I had too much life left to sell my body for cheap. Too smart to cloud my brain with drugs, blah, blah, blah.

Simply because I was young, thankfully, she believed in second chances. I would be escorted to rehabilitation for thirty days. She expected me to clean up my act. Stay in a half-way house for a year afterwards, where I would be on probation.

That meant I had to stay clean, find gainful employment, and basically change the fast life I was living. She promised that if I failed in any way and I landed in jail again, I would be placed in prison.

Police officers escorted me out of the courtroom, placed me in a cell until they completed my paperwork. I wouldn't see Dre again for a while. But from the anger on his face in the courtroom, I didn't want to. Although I was frightened of what he would do when he saw me again, my body relaxed in relief because I would be away from him. Maybe this was my second

chance….................

Ashley

Never thought I would end up in a mental ward. Never thought I would want to die. But the pills and alcohol I took said just that. I was a nobody before. A nobody when I was with my family. A nobody while I was in high school.

But I joined the Army and I became somebody. I had friends. Boys liked me. I was someone. Now what would they think of me? Just a crazy promiscuous drunk, probably. I was in a mental ward. I couldn't believe it. My mind raced. My frustrations and fear spilled over. I opened my mouth and I screamed.........

A nurse opened the door quickly which meant cameras were somewhere. She took me into what appeared to be an eating area. Moved me away from other sleeping patients. Gave me crackers and water. I ate slowly while she watched me. I felt crazy but I was also hungry.

I stared off into space as she explained to me that I was in a mental ward. I already figured that much out. She explained that earlier they had pumped my stomach. They placed me here because I was screaming I wanted to die. It all seemed like a dream.

She asked me why I wanted to die. I continued to stare off into space. Wishing she would just leave me alone. Hoping desperately to wake up from this nightmare. I finished my water and said I wanted to go back to sleep.

She walked me back to the sleeping area and before she closed the door, I softly said *"they raped me, they all raped me"*. I laid back down and went to sleep instantly.

Sunday passed by like a whirlwind. The nurse really did hear what had I whispered the night before. I had given her my consent to report it. They all deserved to pay for what they did to me. The day was filled with doing a rape kit, talking to the military police, talking to the chaplain, and talking to a therapist. The therapist finally asked what I wanted to do.

I didn't understand her question. What did I want to do about what? Them raping me? My best friend deserting me and turning on me? All of these things wanted to come screaming out of my mouth. I really just wanted all of this to be a bad dream but I realized it wasn't. So I asked if I could be taken away from my command for a while since the perpetrators were part of it. I wasn't ready to face anyone.

The next day I was transported to a rehabilitation center, the place my psychiatrist and command recommended since the incident started with underage and binged drinking. I was just happy I wouldn't have to face those accusing, disgusted faces on base. People disgusted me.

Tasha

This will be the second time I popped. I didn't care the last time either. I'm too pretty and classy to pay somebody for a clean sample. Touching someone else's piss is disgusting. Might go back to prison this time because of my big ego. I care but I don't.

I previously served 2 years for what I saw as self-defense. Got off easy because the judge understood his side and mine. So I'm officially an ex-convict. Such an ugly title for such a classy woman. Nothing I can do to change it now. My record is forever dirty. So why in the hell would I care about going back to prison?

I walked into my parole officer's shabby office and plopped down in a raggedy chair that threatened to give in at any moment.

My parole officer, John, sighed in exasperation. "Tasha, I'm going to be honest with you. This is the second drug test you failed and usually that means back to prison. Do you not even care?"

I shrugged my shoulders. "So what's it gonna be, John?"

I dared him to make a decision. I wanted to see if I could call his bluff.

The look on his face screamed frustration. "I know your story. And I empathize with you. Maybe a better lawyer would have kept you out of the system. That's neither here nor there now. The thing is I have to take action on this matter or my job is on the line."

I nodded and waited for him to continue.

He searched my face for any protests. I had none. He had to do what he had to do. I made my choices. I could live with them.

"I've decided to give you one more chance to do this thing right. I'm going to send you to rehab for thirty days."

A million questions ran through my mind. But I just had one important one. "I am transsexual. Will I be with women or men?"

Lorie

They found me. After a week of running, a week of seeing my face on tv, on posters. They found me. This was the longest it had taken them. But eventually I knew they would. I was the poster child. Not the poster child for an angel. No, not like my brother, Christian. I was the poster child of what goes wrong with rich kids.

My parents were wealthy. Not just from their own family inheritances, but from investments and their careers. My mom was a big shot doctor who made house calls to the famous. My dad provided those same people with legal services. He was a lawyer.

Technically their money found me. I am sure they paid the most expensive private investigator. And she earned her wages well. Dirty clothes, dirty hair. I smelled of the piss and trash that surrounded me. They caught me in the midst of boosting my high.

She asked me one question and the look on her face told my 20 year old mind just how serious things were this time. "Your parents are done. Live your life here or go to rehab?"

I stood up and followed her out of the door.

Discussion

- What was your breaking point?

- What was your addiction?

- Do you think these characters went to rehab for the right reasons?

- Why or why not?

- Do you feel you are here for the right reasons?

Chapter Two

Breaking Habits

Counselor (Becky)

I watched the pain in her eyes, saw sweat drip from the tip of her nose, the screams that rose from her throat. She was detoxing. Coming off a high that kept her above the level of her true pain.

And yet the scene did not turn me away. Didn't make me cringe, didn't make me want to reach out and help. Because I had seen this before. Saw my mom come down so bad when she could no longer use her body to barter for drugs.

That's partly why I love what I do. I never had the chance to help my mother. Wasn't old enough to understand what I could do to help. But I learned, researched, and I paid my way through school. So maybe I could save those from the inevitable terrible end if they didn't change. Help them confront their demons like I did mine so they could have a desirable life.

And I had 30 days. 30 short days to help them. But in those 30 days, I promised myself I would do everything I could. I continued to watch this angel's agony…..............

Cheyenne

My first day and my mind is consumed with what Trishton is doing or should I say who. I couldn't help it. I wondered if he was taking this thirty day opportunity to sleep around.

But I have to concentrate. The first day went well. Filled with medical questions, checking out the facility. It was relaxing to get away but then it wasn't. This strange place. Knowing what everyone was here for. Wondering if someone would flip out, if someone was judging me.

But I needed to focus. There were five women in our group. None of them much younger or older than myself. Some on drugs. I actually believe one was born male. Curiosity was killing me as to what brought them to this point.

Focus. I need to focus. We were instructed to write about how we got here and what we wanted from treatment.

I met him at a new duty station. I had a boyfriend. He had a girlfriend. But Trishton was tall, dark, and handsome. His confidence turned me on. His accent kept me on. Long story short, I dumped my boyfriend and fell in love.

Thinking about it now, our relationship started on nights in clubs or hanging out playing cards with alcohol always within reach. Alcohol seemed to make everything easier. Easier to say and easier to do.

I had been in bad relationships before but nothing like this. I did a lot to keep Trishton happy. Things I'm embarrassed to say. I ignored a lot of what he did. Things that made my heart bleed in pain. Two years later, everything begin to boil over. Every pain I held inside exploded. The alcohol kept setting it free.

And yet when I expressed my pains he wanted to leave me and it drove me crazy. All I wanted was for him to sacrifice like I did. But my pains made him leave. Anger consumed me. Alcohol ignited the fire. And I hated him and I loved him.

Everyone saw my pain, my drunkenness, my angry ways. In their minds I was crazy. They didn't know the things he did. In their eyes, he was perfect. And slowly I wanted to die. But

17

not really. I just wanted to be set free. But while the alcohol ignites my pain and Trishton keeps the fire burning, I will forever be insane.

So what do I want? I want to be able to function without the alcohol, express myself without that liquid courage, I want to find my own courage.......

Jennifer

The last few nights have been the easiest to sleep yet the hardest. Embarrassed as the new group of women watched me sweat the drugs out of my body. Watched my body tremble hard. They had given me something to help me through the withdrawals but I still had some withdrawal symptoms. Not enough to put me in a withdrawal room.

I looked at the women in my group. Thought they could never have it as bad as I did. Embarrassed at the thought of revealing what I did for a living. But I needed to focus. Damn, I needed a hit. No, no I don't. But I need a better life even more. Let me concentrate on this assignment.

My family kicked me out so I had nothing. Barely sixteen, living dirty and hungry on the streets. Beyond broke, unable to fix myself up enough to get a job. Survival meant just waking up to see a new day. Dre saved me. He gave me shelter, food, and clothing.

But then I found out what he expected of me in return, my body. The selling of my body ripped away any feelings I had

19

left in me. The drugs boosted me enough to enjoy some pieces of life. But such as everyone in this line of work, being caught was inevitable. The judge had mercy on me and gave me a chance to clean up my act though.

As I sat in jail, I panicked about going to prison, flashes of dreams haunted me. This was not what I wanted. I wanted to be someone's wife, have children, and have the family I never did. I wanted to celebrate Christmas, go to an office job every day, and take care of my family at night. I wanted to enjoy making them breakfast in the mornings.

I want to change my life. I want to become respectable. I want to enjoy life without the need for boosters. I truly want to be happy and free.

Ashley

I was embarrassed. I cried all the time now as images of that night ran through my brain. As my shame echoed down the halls of my barracks. Everyone here knew nothing of my story except my counselor. And yet they knew something was wrong.

My eyes always threatened to overflow. I don't want to talk about what got me here. Not now, maybe not ever. What do I want from here? Right now, just a break from my shame and my unit…................

Tasha

I was used to the stares, the questions. As I introduced myself, I could see the curiosity of all the young women spilling over. Usually my high would make me uncaring, but that was taken from me. But back to this assignment....

I was born male and years later I officially became a woman. Doesn't matter what made me change, but it is who I am now. I've smoked since I can remember. Change can be hard especially when those around you know you were born male.

People ridicule you, insult you, and sometimes assault you. Once I had fully become a woman, I fell in love. Not that earth shaking kind of love but the kind that leaves you floating freely in outer space.

He didn't know my true past but fell in love with who I presented to him. He even proposed. That was the night I told him the truth. And he tried to kill me. Instead I came away with a few bruises and he with broken bones.

I spent time in prison for the assault. And when I came out, the truth about the world left me shattered. People will forever be prejudice and unaccepting. So I smoked.

Now I just want to stay out of prison. It isn't a pretty place. There's no fashionable clothing or hair salons there. The screams at night will leave a person with nightmares for life. And I guess in doing so I need to face the world with a clear head, without the drugs................

Lorie

Hell. That's where I've been for the past two days. They gave me something to help me through the withdrawal. But it didn't help much. Sweat drenched my clothes as I burned up. The wet clothes left me frozen as I quickly cooled down.

I ate, I vomited, I cried, and I screamed. I begged for my mommy and daddy to love me. I told Christian I hated him. Hopefully this hell is almost over. Feels like I'm dying. And they left me in this room to die alone........................

Discussion

- What happened in the last 30 days that led you here?

- What events in your past do you believe led you here? (Relationships with family members, friends, a traumatic event, etc.)

- What do you want from this treatment?

Chapter Three

Dear Self Judgment

The Serenity Prayer

"God, grant me the serenity to accept the things I cannot change, courage to change the things I can, and the wisdom to know the difference."

Counselor: Becky

The hardest part of our setbacks is often accepting the things we have done. People judge, whether mentally or in spoken words. People will push their opinions on others.

People will remind you of what you have done. Sometimes because they hurt so much from what has happened that they want to continue to hurt you in return. Other times it is because they find faults within themselves and in order to mask their faults, they choose to continuously shine light on yours.

We cannot change what we have done. We cannot change others' views, actions, or reactions. The only person we can control is ourselves. We must learn and grow from our past so that it does not affect our present or future.

Often that comes with acknowledging who we were and what we have done. Then we must change our thinking and become who we want to be. We control our destinies.

Cheyenne

Dear Lie,

You said that all you wanted was love, spawning from the lack of love in your past. But somehow you created a monster and went through years of love that didn't last.

You blamed yourself consistently for things you could not control. You loved a man obsessively and that same love bit you tenfold.

You cannot recreate the love you wanted from a father or a mother. You cannot expect the ideal love by not looking any further.

You allowed someone to hurt you without speaking up. And in turn that silence had you drinking quickly from a cup.

Love yourself, Cheyenne, love yourself, like no one ever will. Explore yourself, girl, amaze yourself, and life dreams may be fulfilled.

Better to wait patiently for someone who appreciates me than cry in a damp dark room. Because if you keep traveling this road, your heart and life will be consumed...........

Jennifer

Dear Family,

You left me, you left me, you left me out in this crazy world. Knowing I was just an unruly teen, just a teen-aged girl. Exploring the world, exploring who I am. Forgetting consequences, just not giving a damn.

You were supposed to lock me up, you were supposed to chew me out. Rather than leave me, I'd have enjoyed your screams and shouts. But instead I grew up much faster, did things a young woman should never do. I opened up my body, just to start life anew.

I was supposed to go to homecoming, I was supposed to go to prom. Mom, you were supposed to take pictures and dad would tag along.

What am I doing, running down a list of should have, could have, would have been. This is now and my destruction has to end. I see a young woman in a dress. Which nursery theme, which dinner party is her stress.

It's her little girl's first day of school. The young woman lays down laws, she lays down rules. Because one day her little girl will be as unruly just as she. But instead of abandoning her, they'll just disagree.

And this woman will kneel down and pray, for her little girl to change her ways. And the girl will be protected from a young life of sin. The girl will be shown new beginnings before she sees her end........

Tasha

I used to wonder who I am. I've been bounded by society's expectations of who we should be. Thrown to the wayside are the simple things of humanity such as loving others as one expects to be loved, respecting self as we respect those surrounding us, and treating one another in a manner that does not cause intentional harm mentally or physically.

These things are the basics, before one can lend a hand, before one can ask for a hand. Without these things, coexisting peacefully cannot happen. Yet people focus on appearance, race, sex, sexuality, and religion.

Obama, Bush, Hitler, Saddam, they all led countries. Bill Gates and Oprah became billionaires. The Pope and TD Jakes became famous religious leaders. Rupaul, Frank Ocean, Ellen DeGeneres, the list goes on. People who will be forever known for the things they have contributed to this world.

They all made some type of difference regardless of their sexual preference, religion, or beliefs. They made a major impact on someone. Clothing, food products, services, all used

32

by everyone every day. Made by people from different cultures, different sex, and different religions. None of this made a difference on how they contributed to the world.

Yet, there are people, will always be people, who are too blinded by sexuality, race, and religion, to truly appreciate the valuable minds that exist in this world. Those people are ignorant. Why? Because if they were discriminated against because of what is called "social norms", they would be angry.

I could go on and on for centuries about the injustices of this world. But it's not going to change people. Therefore I have to change me. From this day forth, people will know who I am, who I was, where I came from. Whether they choose to accept me or not is up to them. In the end, they will suffer the loss of not being able to socialize with such a great, beautiful, loving person.

Ashley

Accept the things I cannot change? Change the things I can? When I'm surrounded by a million folks who just don't give a damn. Destroying nations, destroying freedoms. Wondering who we can trust when the innocence becomes pure evil?

They don't know pain until they experience it themselves. They don't understand needs until they need some help. Amazed at the expense people will pay to destroy another life. Amazed at the evil greed with no sacrifice.

Accept the things I cannot change you say, change the things I can. I just find that hard to do when no one else gives a damn.

Lorie

I wasn't born poor. I was born into wealth. I don't know the feeling of wanting, but I do know the feeling of death. Because what I wanted was handed to me, but what I needed cannot be.

I'm sorry I wasn't born a boy, it's just something I cannot change. To carry my father's legacy, so I carried his name in shame. They say accept the things you cannot change and that's exactly what I did. So I focused on the things I could and I finessed it.

Now I always get the attention that I need, because of the reputation my parents want for this family. I wish they could understand all my hurt, all my pain. Then I wouldn't have to live life this way. Death just continues to knock at my door because of the loveless life I do not adore.

Accepting the things I cannot change, means they will continue to hold their heads in shame.

Discussion

- Did the angels grasp the concept of the serenity prayer?
  Who did or didn't? Why?

- What are your thoughts on the serenity prayer?

- What does it mean to you?

- Can you relate to any of the angels in this chapter? If so,
  why?

Chapter Four

Wanting

Becky

We often ask ourselves these questions:

Why don't we get what we want?

Why doesn't anyone listen to me and understand me?

Shouldn't they have already known from my actions, reactions, or lack thereof?

Why aren't they listening to me?

Often we feel this way because of a breakdown in communication. We cannot always predict what another person is thinking or what they want. Often without proper communication, we can only make assumptions. These assumptions can be based on what we think is best, what seems adequate for us. Our assumptions can often totally miss the target of someone else's needs if it isn`t communicated properly.

So how do we communicate? Are we passive, aggressive, or passive-aggressive when we communicate? What do these things even mean?

A passive person can also be considered submissive. This is the person who may not speak up for themselves. They may even speak up but when another person disagrees they may go along with the other person's idea rather than stick to their decisions.

The aggressive person is often forceful and hostile. They usually communicate in such a way that often leads to confrontation. Their approach often suggests that they are ready to argue and fight and they often use techniques such as humiliation and verbal abuse to achieve their goal. They usually don't take the other person's thoughts or feelings into consideration.

The passive-aggressive person is usually somewhere in between the previous two. This person may feel hostile and upset but expresses it in subtle ways while seemingly agreeing with the subject at hand.

The idea communicator is assertive. They express their needs in a way that shows respect to others while not sacrificing their own needs. They express their needs and wants in a clear manner without disrespecting the needs and wants of others.

What is a need or want that you need to communicate to someone else? How will you communicate it to them? How will they react?

Cheyenne

All of my life I have been abandoned. My mother placed men before her children. My first love broke up with me. My second love cheated and lied to me after I had given him most of me.

My grandparents placed their blood relatives before my mother's children because my mom was adopted. My mom left us with our grandparents to travel with her 4th husband. Everyone has always left. Doesn't true love never abandon, never hurt?

Trishton, I have loved you with everything I have. Everything you've wanted I have done regardless of the pain it has caused, physical and emotional. When I knew you cheated, I pretended to believe you when you said it was a lie. When you told me if I loved you I would do it, I did it. When you dictated what I wore, what I ate, I followed because I love you.

What I need is the type of love I have given. I need love that doesn't make me fear you will leave me at the drop of a dime. I need love that is open and honest and respects my wants and needs. I need love that says I am worthy rather than compare me to others. I need the love that accepts my individuality. I need love in the form of affection. A small gesture such as a random kiss, a surprise date, a texts randomly saying "I love you".

I want to be the number one love in someone's life. I don't want to question everything someone says fearing it is a lie. In my world, love is honest. A lie only prolongs the damage the truth could cause. I want to communicate in a way that, when we are done, we both feel content with the decisions made. I want to be truly loved.

How will he react?

He will talk until I no longer wish to listen and I just concede to what he wants. He will point out all of the things he has done for me that no one else has. He will say obviously he isn't what I want and threaten to leave me when he knows I want him to stay. He will guilt trip me into thinking I am overreacting.

Jennifer

Before I can attempt to build a new relationship with my family again, I want to change my life now. I fear Dre. I fear that he may become violent however I must get away. Even if I never get to truly express myself to him, I want this conversation to play again and again in my head to remind myself of what I need and that I plan to get there.

Dre, when I had no place to go, no place to eat, you rescued me. You saved me from starvation and I am grateful. However, when I imagined making my own money and building a life for myself, I did not imagine the hurtful things I would have to do to get to that point.

Sleeping with men every night who used my body, without any regards as to who I was or how I felt, was shameful. My skin crawled as I allowed my mind to take me everywhere except for what I was doing. The love I assumed you had for me was consumed by your need for the money.

Lavish clothes and a hot meal dimmed in comparison to what I expected love to be. A person who loves does not intentionally allow the humiliation and misuse of the person they love.

I no longer want to use my body to make money and survive. I want to work a normal 9 to 5, even if it is minimum wage, to make an honest living. At least then I will be able to look at myself in the mirror every morning.

I want to finish school and maybe go to college. I want the next man who lays with me to be my husband. A husband who will love and respect me.

I understand that breaking away from you will mean the loss of significant money. But you have others. If you want to see me succeed as much as you say you do, you'd let me go and allow me to fulfill my dreams.

My body will eventually grow old and tired. I want to look back at my life when I am older and be able to say "I've made mistakes but I changed and have lived the life I wanted". I am just asking that you let me go peacefully.

How will he react?

Simple. He will be angry and threaten to kill me. He will point out how he saved me from being homeless. More than likely he will hit me. He will say I will not make it without him.

Ashley

Brittany, what happened to you? Where were you in my time of need? All of you, we went on hikes together, complained about our leaders together, when someone needed a dollar we lent it even though we were broke. So what did I do to make you shame me, to make you violate me, to make you abandon me?

I need an answer so I know what I did wrong. I don't understand. Do you think I am ugly? Do you really think that less of me? I want to make things right. I want to hear you apologize and say you didn't mean it, that it was the alcohol.

Please…......just say the alcohol made things go too far….........

Tasha

I have been judged for so long that you should understand when I don't reveal everything about me upon first meeting. I have been verbally abused, gay bashed, and even assaulted for who I am. When I met you, you found me beautiful. You loved the way I carried myself, exuding confidence. You liked my sexy voice, the way I laughed.

I found myself so in love with you. You liked me for who I am. And when we spoke of committing, I should have told you then. But I needed to know how committed you were before I revealed my true self. You were my first after my full change. My first love, my first lover.

We played house and I loved it. Watching you fix me a surprise breakfast, rubbing my feet as you watched your football game. I was honestly surprised when you finally proposed to me. I knew then that you were truly in love and that it was time to share all of me.

I had never seen such anger and hurt in your face when I told you I was born male. I didn't understand how you could fall in love and turn it into hatred with just a small piece of information.

What I am trying to communicate to you is that I am sorry. Sorry for betraying you. I didn't mean to hurt you. I just wanted, needed, true love regardless of my past. What I need is forgiveness from you. I need to know that you don't hate me because I don't want to go on in life knowing the one person I truly loved truly hates me.

Lorie

Mom, Dad. I never intended to start using. I never wanted it to consume me. But when I felt that high, everything that hurt simply disappeared. And I kept chasing that high.

The only time it felt like anyone noticed me was when I disappeared for days. But I'm alive, I'm your child just as much as Christian is. I'm just as smart and I can be just as successful.

What I need is your support. I need your affection and your love. I need to know that you value me just as much as you do Christian.

I need to know that you think I am worthy of your time, of your thoughts, or your affection. I need you to acknowledge that I am an important part of the family.

And if you can't, I cannot guarantee that I won't continue to disgrace this family because I need you to know I am part of you, whether in a good way or a bad way. The choice is yours.

How they will react....

They will probably state they have provided all the
necessities in life to me, that I have grown up with an advantage
and am being spoiled.

Discussion

- Discuss how each of these girls communicated and how they may communicate differently.

- Do you feel any of them will be better off not communicating, taking into account the reactions that they expect? Why?

- How do you communicate?

- Talk about a time that you felt you didn't communicate well and then communicate it in an assertive manner.

Chapter Five

"Feelings, Thoughts, Behavior

Becky

You ever heard of someone who wasn't sick but believed so intensely that they were that they actually begin feeling symptoms? Our thoughts can also cause the same symptoms. Our thoughts become feelings that often lead to certain behaviors. We start to believe our thoughts although they may not necessarily be reality.

For instance, after a well-rested weekend it is now Monday morning. You slept a peaceful 8 hours. Now it is time to go to work. When you wake up your thought is that you're so tired that you won't be productive today. You begin to move sluggishly, you feel mentally tired and foggy, and you start yawning a lot. You now feel what you were thinking.

When you get to work, you move slowly through your tasks, you have no sense of urgency. You don't attempt to concentrate during the meeting. This is because from the moment you woke up you already thought you were too tired to concentrate and begin to feel that way. Your negative thinking has now become negative feelings and negative behaviors.

But what if I told you that the cycle of thoughts, feelings, and behaviors can be broken? That even if you had a negative thought you could change it before it becomes a feeling and behavior? That even if you reach the negative feeling you can still change the behavior?

For instance, using the same example from above. You woke up and thought "I am so tired". You then decide to turn on some music that pumps energy through your veins as you take a hot shower.

Not just any music, not the music that makes you sad. But those few songs on your play list that say you are the greatest, you rule the world, you can do anything you want. These words become thoughts in your head. You DO rule the world! You begin singing and dancing in the shower and you wash away those sleepy eyes.

This one action wakes you up and you feel ready for the day. The positive energy from the music and shower has really energized you. Now you begin to feel excited about going to accomplish some major tasks at work. You keep the music going in your car and you are feeling hyped. You get to work and you are just completing task left and right.

Do you see what a difference changing your routine made? Instead of wallowing in the feeling of exhaustion, you used a method of relaxation (music) to inspire you. Name a few times when you had an automatic thought that led to negative feelings and behaviors.

Cheyenne

I see him looking at another woman while walking through the mall. My breasts and my behind aren't nearly as curvaceous as those he sees. He doesn't love me because I am not good enough. My body feels as if it has turned cold, my eyes begin to burn.

I tense up. I begin to cry. I am sad, depressed, and angry. I take all of his things and throw them over the balcony. The military police are called.

The next time, he comes to my room and tells me it is over, seriously this time. His voice is void of emotions that I feel. He should hurt like I do. I cry, I scream. He leaves as if I mean nothing.

I need to feel numb. These feelings are too overwhelming. I begin drinking straight from the bottle. My tears dry and I hate him. I am furious at him. How dare he take, take, and take then discard me at his will? I go to his living space and throw everything he gave me on his car as I continue to drink from the bottle. The military police are called. They confront me. I scream that I want to die.

Jennifer

My parents said I couldn't go to the party because there would be drinking and drugs. They don't trust me. They never let me go anywhere. They want me to be just as miserable as they are, bored and cooped up in the house.

My body tenses. I grab the skimpiest clothes I can find. I defiantly walk out the front door with no jacket on. I feel free from their supervision. I feel misunderstood. My parents don't know me at all.

Years later, I head out to the job. I am disgusting, just a human body to be used. I need to be numbed to get through this. I hate myself. Afterwards, I look in the mirror at myself. I hate the person I see.

I am not numb enough. I slide my stash from my dress and take a long hit and place the rest back. I go back out. He makes me an offer and I hop into the car. He's an undercover cop. I am going to jail.

Ashley

I woke up alone. I'm depressed. I play ""It's A Lonely Day" by System of a Down. I brush my teeth and run my hands through my hair to put it up. I mean what's the point of putting in any effort into my appearance? I grabbed a bottle of water, take a sheet and hang it over the window so sunlight won't come in and hop back in bed. I get back up and put the song on repeat. I lay back in bed and cry until I fall asleep. I missed phone calls and texts. There was a surprise party for veterans at the recreation center. My name was drawn for a prize, but I wasn't there to claim it.

Scene change. Its pay day but I hate my life. No one is truly my friend, I think to myself as I wake up. I will always be alone. I throw on sweats and head to the casino. I turn off my phone. I become so hypnotized by the slot machines. My mind isn't focused on anything but winning. I hit the ATM again and again. Before I know it, the bank says I have insufficient funds. Now I am broke for another two weeks and alone. I go back home and cry myself to sleep.

Tasha

I wake up and know I am all woman. When I met him, he was the man women dream about. Handsome, smart, employed, and had his own. But men like this don't date other men. They tend to be homophobic. They tend to look down on men who become women or who simply like men. My love and lust wanted to keep him here. Fear kept me from telling him I was born male. And I let days then months pass. I let joy override fear. Until the day he asked me to be his wife. I let down my walls. And I told him. Hell has never seen such rage........

My arrival here. Ever since I can remember I have woken up with the same routine. This morning was no different. My alarm went off and as I rolled over to smack it off, my first thought was I need to smoke a blunt real quick, ease myself into the day. As I puffed away, it hit me. I had to see my parole officer. My shoulders tensed. I could feel a headache coming on. The parole officer would always be my reminder. Screw it. I puffed harder. Time to go fail the drug test. I wondered how much time I would spend in the joint this time.

Lorie

We were at a party. I over hear my parents bragging about how my brother is doing well following in my father's footsteps. He'll make a great lawyer someday. They are such proud parents. They don't know I exist. I can't get their attention. I am sad, hurt, angry, lonely, frustrated. I feel my face turn red, my skin burn hot as the couple glances at me. I am burning with shame. They notice that my parents don't mention me. I walk away.

I would never normally hang with this group but their parents dote on them. The fancy type. They invite me upstairs where I know the drugs are flowing. The need drives me to believe that if I overdose parents will notice me. They will love me. They will have no choice. I do something they called meth. It was first time but I keep going like it's the 100th time. I fade out. I blink in and out. Moments of consciousness allows me to see the paramedics. Moments of consciousness allows me to see the worried face of my parents. As I slip into a coma, I smile. They notice me now.

Discussion

- Identify the event, thoughts, and feelings each woman experienced.

- What was the subsequent behavior and outcome?

- What thoughts could have changed the feelings and behaviors?

- What were some events and/or thoughts that led to negative feelings and behaviors in your life?

- What could you have thought or done differently to break the negative cycle?

- If broken, what would have been the alternate outcome?

Chapter Six

Investing

Becky

Some people succeed by being lucky enough to be in the right place at the right time under the right circumstances. But the majority of people have to plan, re-plan, and revamp that plan again. Temptation and fate threatens.

A tempting alternative presents itself that threatens to take you off of your path. An uncontrollable event that was totally unexpected happens. You must choose, you must sacrifice, and you must keep going in one direction or another. It can be stressful. But resilience and planning against life's whirlwinds will take you to the finish line.

With everything we do in life we ultimately plan no matter how big or small. When you wake up in the morning you must decide whether to go to work or stay home. That determines if you get dressed and how you dress. If you go to work, you decide which route to take. If you stay home, you think about what you will do all day. But you take action either way. These are short quick plans.

Long term plans actually require a bit more thought. For example, you are going to have a baby. This will increase your expenses. Before that baby is born, you budget your expenses. You choose daycare based on location, pricing, and reputation. You find a backup sitter just in case. This is planning for the long term. Planning for the ""what ifs".

Often when we don't plan, we make rash decisions. This often leaves us with outcomes we don't desire. Making a plan is the first step in fulfilling a plan. As a reminder to us and to track our progress, it is often best to write our plan down.

We must then stick to the plan and have alternatives to compensate for the unexpected events. We must remind ourselves of our plan and stay focused on the outcome we desire. Most importantly we must take action because writing down a beautiful plan only ends up being a nicely designed piece of paper unless we follow through with it.

Cheyenne

My long term goal is to become a certified public accountant. It'll take at least five years to complete my Master's degree. I'll need to gain two years of experience under a Certified Public Accountant but that will be difficult. There aren't certified accountants in the military. I work anywhere from 9-24 hours a day.

When will I be able to go to school? Will I be allowed to take vacation time to gain experience? How will I find a CPA if I'm overseas?

First things first. I need to go to school. My enrollment is my initial short term goal. I can research some of the online programs many people talk about. I know the military will pay for the tuition for a certain amount of classes.

That's what I will do first. Go see an education specialist, find a suitable school, and figure out how to complete the paperwork required. I can start with one or two classes to ease myself in.

I can start earning hours towards licensing once I graduate with my Bachelor's. If I am overseas, I can request leave if I find a certified accountant to let me train a few hours a week. If not, I'll have to wait until I return to the United States and take the leave. Or who knows, maybe I won't be in the military by then and it'll be easier. In the mean time I can work on my Master's degree.

Jennifer

I want to stop selling my body. That is my short term goal. I want to work a regular job, have my own place, and finish school. At least get my GED so maybe I'll have a chance at college. But first I need a place to stay because I don't have my own. I'll need to check with my counselor to see if I can stay in an Adult Community. It may have already been set-up through the court requirements.

I need to stay surrounded by sober people. I can get cleaned up and start working at a small job even if it pays minimum wage. Something is better than nothing. Maybe within a month, I'll save enough money to buy more decent clothes and pay for my own public transportation. I can get on the internet and research GED programs in the area. Go to school during the day and work a few hours at night before curfew. First step, speak to my counselor about an adult community and donated clothing. Once settled, I will begin my job and GED program search.

Ashley

      Surprisingly, once I entered into the Army I saw myself retiring as a Sergeant Major. I love the training, the deployments, seeing the world. I want to be a drill sergeant. Molding young female soldiers. But I need to get my training scores up, start studying, and go on a few meritorious promotion boards. I'll need to get promoted so I can be a drill sergeant.

      I also plan to go to school in the meantime for business, that way when I retire I have something to fall back on. I will follow through with my education office to see how I can be enrolled. My first step is to get back into conditioning my body so I can get higher scores on my physical fitness tests. Start a physical fitness regimen. The energy and rush always leaves me feeling refreshed.

Tasha

No surprise here. I want to get into the make-up, hair, and fashion business. Eventually I want to style big artists like Beyoncé or super models like Tyra. Unfortunately, school costs money. I've been living off of a trust fund these past few years and have budgeted as such. Maybe in order to have funds for school, I can work during the day and go to school at night. But I need to stay clean first. Can't do cosmetology in the pen.

I'll need to start job hunting. I hear it's hard with a record but if I don't give up, maybe I'll find something. There may be programs out there that help those who have previously been convicted find gainful employment. I need to start searching for cosmetologist courses. Find out the costs, see where I need to cut expenses in order to pay for the courses.

Lori

I want to go to college. Partly to prove to my parents that I can do something with my life. Partly because even if they don't accept me, I can build a life of my own so that I am independent. I'll be able to raise a family where my children all know they are loved. Maybe I'll be a psychiatrist. Help women such as this group. Help ease their minds and their pains. It'll be so expensive but I am sure my parents will pay for it. It's going to take a lot of work.

I'll need to do the SAT exam first though. My brain may be fried, I'll probably need to take a preparation course. Start applying to some universities. Maybe I'll go to a school away from my family, so I don't have constant reminders of what I don't have. Start somewhere fresh, where people barely know me or my parents. So I can be my own person.

Discussion

- Do you think the characters have good plans? Why or why not?

- Do you think their plans are reasonable and achievable?

- What do you want to do with your life?

- What are your goals and what plans do you have to achieve them (short term and long term)?

- Who can you reach out to for assistance with your goals?

Chapter Seven

Risky Investments

Becky

Sometimes unpreventable events happen. You get a flat tire. Your electricity bill is double the amount you planned it to be. You get sick and you miss out on wages due to your absence from work. Most of the time, these are things you can't prevent. You can take medicine, you can drive on decent roads, and you can turn your heat down but ultimately these things could happen even with the preventative measures.

On the other hand, there are also preventable events that happen. You have no gas because you spent your last $20 on lottery tickets. You're unable to pay your bills because you took leisure time off of work, knowing that you needed the hours.

You received a zero on your homework assignment because you procrastinated. Even when you knew the due date, you chose to go party under the assumption that the teacher would just reduce your grade for lateness. Unfortunately he was very unforgiving.

When we make a plan, we cannot predict everything that will happen. But we can give ourselves options for the "just in case". For example, placing funds into your savings account for emergency situations such as your car needing repairs will decrease the stress when the situation does occur.

We also need to recognize alternatives that could sway us from the path we choose to take. Recognizing these temptations will not only prepare us to fight against them but also allows us to think about how far we may fall from our goal if we do allow ourselves to be swayed.

For example, you need to pay your tuition for school. Your other option would be to spend the money partying. If you stay focused on going to school, you would purchase your book and pay your tuition right away. If you choose to party, you'll be forced to drop a course and ultimately take longer to finish your degree program. You have to also hope that the course you drop isn't a prerequisite to other courses because then you'll be further delayed.

For a moment, let's acknowledge events, both predictable and unpredictable, that will prevent us or delay us from achieving our goals.

Cheyenne

I've been with Trishton for the past two years. I have alienated my family and friends for him. His friends became my friends. He works with me, in the same unit, in the same office. I am going to want to run back to him. I want his companionship. I desire his touch. Although times were bad, it was better than nothing. If I see him with other women I will get angry. My anger will possibly drive me to drink and act out.

Being lonely will tempt me to drink my sorrows away. Hanging out with friends who drink will tempt me to drink. Most of the people I know drink whether they are relaxing at home or partying. They will offer to buy me drinks. Drinking will lead to hangovers and bad actions.

If I am hung-over or in trouble, I won't be completing my homework assignments and will fail school. If I fail, I will have to pay the tuition back and I don't have that type of money. It could put me into debt that may be hard to get out of.

If I go back to him I will more than likely drink and party again. The outcome will be the same. I will act irrationally and become distracted from school. If I continue acting out, the

Marine Corps could discharge me not only early but also dishonorably. I would lose my benefits to include education benefits.

Jennifer

Dre might find me. He may want to punish me for losing so much money. I may be so scared that I do exactly what he says and start earning his money back by prostituting again. If I go back into that, I'll more than likely use to make it through the streets at night.

If I don't find a place and clothing, I'll be homeless and improperly dressed to work at a decent place. If I am homeless, I would be tempted to go back to Dre for shelter. If I do find a place but lack clothing and transportation, I will be tempted to sell myself again in order to get money for my needs. This will lead back to using and I may find myself in a place where I can't revert back to a clean life.

The job market may be tough. I may have to work hard and be underpaid. I may sell again to earn money or use to cope with the stressors of work. If any of this happens, school will definitely be postponed or even become a lost dream.

Ashley

My goals will be delayed until I get to my new unit. I'll be consumed with moving and testifying. I'm terrified of testifying. I may be tempted to drink to calm my nerves. If I drink, I'll become depressed and want to consume more than I should. People will probably shun me. They do that a lot when there is a rape case. People will accuse me of being a whore or accuse me of asking for it.

I will feel isolated and alone with no one to talk to. I may want alcohol to cope with the loneliness. I could be in trouble for under-age drinking. I could lose my rank and pay. That will demotivate me. It may hold me up from leaving my current duty station even longer.

Tasha

My past will haunt me. I will want to wake up and smoke out of habit and from the temptation to relax myself the old way. Seeing my parole officer once a week will remind me that I have lost the one I loved. It will remind me that I did serve time in prison.

I may become depressed about being lonely and may use as a distraction. Finding a job may be difficult with a record. I could become discouraged if I apply and don't ever get hired.

Whether I do or do not find a job, I will need to manage my money. I may not have enough savings to pay for tuition. I hear it is hard to get a student loan with a record. I will have to choose between my living needs and tuition if I am unable to make extra income. Ultimately, my living needs would win and I may become depressed from not achieving my goals.

Lorie

My family may decide that they don't trust me to be away at school on my own. They may think that they are wasting money by sending me off to college. They may continue to ignore me which would tempt me to use and take my mind elsewhere especially during the holidays.

My family may even warn the school about me before I arrive based on my previous behavior and not who am becoming. This may tarnish my reputation at the school before I can build one on my own. That would depress and anger me and I may be tempted to use to cope.

If my parents don't support me, it may be hard to find a job and make enough to pay for school. I may make friends at college who use. I may begin feeling cravings and be tempted to use. I may not be strong enough to turn away. I may not even make friends at school. I may not have a support system.

Discussion

- What are some things that may tempt you to stray off of your path?

- What are some things that may happen that you cannot prevent? (Take into account sobriety, family, friends, your living situation, and financial situation)

Chapter Eight

Decreasing the Risks

Becky

Now that you are aware of the temptations you may face and the unplanned events that may occur think about how you are going to handle them. How do you fight that temptation to party instead of purchasing your textbook? What will keep you from taking that drink or using again?

This is where a plan must be created within a plan. Some people have to make a choice and can often call someone who will dissuade them from doing something they may regret. But what if no one is available to talk to?

Sometimes we must make ourselves reminders as to where we have been and where we do not want to return. It can be something as simple as leaving ourselves little notes around the house with affirmations on them such as "you can do this"" or "stay focused". We could also find another healthy activity to distract us until the temptation wanes. We may read a book or exercise.

We may also choose to attend a meeting such as AA to receive support. It may not be your usual meeting but any group who understands the temptation out there and can give you support will suffice. Ultimately we want to participate in an activity that requires a lot of mental effort but not so much effort that we become frustrated.

Cheyenne

There is no way to avoid Trishton because he works in the same area that I do. However, knowing that everyone will know what transpired and that I ended up with the incident going in my record, I will have to remain professional. Just knowing that everyone is watching me for any reactions will definitely keep me aware of where I am.

If I get lonely, I can definitely go home on the weekends. I only stay about 3 hours away and can spend time with my family. That's a good idea because I've neglected them during my relationship.

During the week, I can start my writing again and school work will also take up much of my time. Maybe I can get back into the reading that I used to do a lot. I need to do my best to avoid him during my off time so that I am not tempted to question him about being with me or anyone else for that matter. I may begin to make friends with some of the women in my unit since my time won't be so consumed by him.

I can also begin a better workout program to improve my physical fitness scores. This will also take up some of my off time. And of course, I can call you ladies if you all desire or make contact with those in my home AA group. That way I'll have a few people to call when I am tempted to drink or make the wrong decision that will lead to drinking.

Jennifer

I am sure Dre will find me if he wants to. It's probably the best idea to go to a group facility in another city that way I can really start fresh. I won't know so many people who may assume I am the same person I was before I left. I will also have to adjust to the bare minimum in life due to the fact that I won't have steady income yet. Even if I can't find an adult facility, I can look into staying at a women's shelter for a few days.

I can also look into resources that help those who are trying to change their lives such as myself. I know outpatient treatment will definitely serve as a reminder as to what I do not want to return to and how I can remain focused.

If I feel the urge to go back to the old me, I can always go to a local library and use the computer. I hear there are some chat rooms out there for those who are addicts. Maybe being able to vent and talk to someone will encourage me to stay on my path. School is also something that will keep me occupied and maybe I can try picking up an exercise routine like running.

I used to enjoy drawing and painting. Maybe I can find some really cheap materials and get back into that habit. I find it very relaxing and it also uses a lot of my time and mental

capacity.

Ashley

I am still adjusting to the fact that many people will probably shun me when I return. I think it may be best if I get into counseling and then continue once I get to my new duty station. This will ultimately help me vent.

I can also start planning my new move. That will also consume much of my time as I pack and gather information on the new location I will be in.

I can spend time communicating via email with the education counselors over there so I can get a head start on enrolling into classes.

This will also be the opportune time to go see a physical fitness coach at the gym and start my workout regimen. I know the gym offers free consultations there and will assess how fit you are now and show you exercises to improve. I can also place a lot of time into studying Army knowledge for the meritorious boards. I think all of these things will definitely keep me occupied until I can start fresh in a new location.

Tasha

I think I like Ashley's idea. I definitely want to enroll in some ongoing counseling to further address many of the past issues I carry with me. Maybe as I continue to talk about them, my mental load will be lightened.

I can also attend the recovery meetings. Enrolling in school and taking on a part time job will definitely keep me busy and occupied. I may also look into maybe joining a fashion design or makeup artist type association. That way I can network and possibly make new friends as well.

Lori

I think I need to begin building a new network of friends. In the meantime, follow on counseling will also be good for me as well. It will allow me to dig deeper into the issues I've been holding onto. I can only do what is in my power to mend my relationship with my immediate family.

However, I can begin reaching out to other family members more and enjoying them. I also need to attend addict meetings. I believe being surrounded by people who have abstained from use will keep me encouraged. I hear often you can partner up with an addict who has a lot of clean time under their belt and they will mentor you.

Discussion

- What do you think of the angels' plans?

- Can any of them improve their plans? How so?

- What are your plans to decrease the risk of relapsing and falling back into old habits?

Chapter Nine

Affirmations

Becky

Your first question may be what is an affirmation? An affirmation is a declaration or statement of belief. The best thing we can do is make positive affirmations. We know our strengths and we know our weaknesses. We know what we can overcome.

Look at how far we've already made it. You've already openly addressed that there is a problem in your life. It takes courage to do that as many people live in a denial. You've even went as far as to state the goals that you do have and even made a plan. You're already ahead of the game.

We have to remember that we control our destinies. Yes, external factors may take us on detours but overall our strength, our courage, and ability to keep pushing will allow us to achieve goals that we never imagined we could. But keep in mind that even when the going gets tough, you have to remember who you are.

Are you strong? Are you an achiever? Do you have something to give to this world? No matter what you think your answers are to these questions, I'm going to tell you that, yes, you are all of these things. You are a discovered angel. You were lost and now you have found yourself, you have discovered the things you want to change, and you have discovered where you want to go.

The discovery is great. The feeling can be one of peace, joy, and/or happiness. I encourage you to write a letter or a poem to yourself. Affirm who you are and the things you plan to do. Then I'll mail it to you. So when you get home, you'll have a reminder. That you are strong, that you can do whatever you put your mind to, and you can do it without using or being destructive.

Cheyenne

Hello Shy.

You've come a long way. You've been gone for a long time. So this letter is to tell you the things that have been on my mind.

You fell down, you fell down hard. Wasn't as simple as scraping a knee.

You had to better yourself with some mental surgery.

You discovered the beautiful person that you are and the great things you can achieve.

Now you're a discovered angel and I know your strength will turn those goals into reality.

You're not weak and you deserve to be treated with respect.

You just continue to grow, don't quit, because this life isn't done with you yet.

I see you being the chief financial officer of your company.

Again, I say, many times, I know you will achieve.

Don't let that bottle destroy all the things that you have changed.

Don't let your sunshine be destroyed by someone else's rain.

Continue to fight, continue to fight.

You discovered angel, you.

Let me watch you grow and your dreams will continue to come

true.

Jennifer

What's up, Jen? Right now you're feeling free.

From that disgusted life you lived, and now you are me.

A discovered angel that rose from the depths of hell

A discovered angel who knows that I will do well

Don't let them do it again, don't let them be a part of your pain

Demand respect, forget the sex, and make the world remember
your name

Jennifer, it is, standing confident, strong, and proud

Resilient, blessed, and purposeful resting on a peaceful cloud

You can and will do all the things you said you would

And at times you may fall, at times you'll be misunderstood

But those things happen in life but you won't allow it to be a
distraction

A degree, a job, a happy life, and you the main attraction

95

Keep pushing, keep pushing

You better not stop

Because your pride, your self-respect is sometimes all you've

got

Ashley

Sweet, sweet, Ashley. Always with good intentions

But bad things have happened, some things best not mentioned

But you are not who they tried to make you out to be

You will show those foolish devils that you're just not that weak

You won't let them bring you down into their dreadful pit

They'll watch you in envy as you succeed and you'll enjoy

every minute of it

This period in your life was just a setback

Now you're ready for the biggest comeback

You discovered angel you

You have so impressed me

With your courage, with your new smile, with your resiliency

Keep it up, keep standing strong

Continue to do well

And all those who try to get in the way

May they all go to hell

Tasha

Hey, Tash. You're a woman, I hear your roar. (I'm laughing to myself). Girl, you know you're much better than what you've been doing. You say you want to be a major designer and make-up artist so what the hell are you doing.

I know you better be enrolling in school or have already done so. And if you haven't found a job yet, keep on pushing. It's going to happen.

And in the midst of this if you're just sitting around twiddling your thumbs, stop twiddling. You told me you were going to join an association dealing with make-up, hair and designing. So get off of your cute little tush and start searching. And then actually go to the meeting.

Don't worry about those judging you. They don't know you or your life story and frankly it's none of their business. You do what you have to do and keep pushing. You don't want to end up back in prison. Girl, the way your hair and nails are done up now will be so raggedy up in there.

Okay, okay, I'm going to stop being long winded. All I wanted to do is remind you that you are strong. Don't let the drugs tempt you back into giving up your freedom and clouding up your mind. You're strong and very creative. You can do so much in life with that. No, you WILL do so much in life with that.

So get off of your cute behind and get to it, chick!

Lorie

Lorie. Wake up!! If you're sleep get out of that bed. You have stuff to do. You've been in a dream for too long. Don't you remember you discovered yourself about 2 or 3 weeks ago? You didn't discover yourself for nothing. Did you begin enrolling in school?

It doesn't matter whether your parents said they would foot the bill or not. Remember you said you were going to do it anyway and I'm seriously holding you to that. You might even meet a cute guy, hehehehe.

Anyway, with the parents you have and the things you have been through. You have to have a lot of strength. Because you survived and are still surviving. But now you know surviving just isn't good enough. You have to live!!!! Live for you.

Now there's girls out here who need you. They need to hear your story. They need you to help them get through this just like Becky did for you. You got this. You're so intelligent and luckily, pretty, and wealthy. That doesn't hurt, lol!

But no, see you in school, at least that's where we better be

headed!

Discussion

- How do you feel about their letters or poems to themselves?

- Take a moment and write a letter or poem to yourself with your affirmations.

Chapter Ten

Spread Your Wings

Becky

It's that time, discovered angels. You have been in this safe place for a great deal of time. But now it's time to prove to yourself that all of the changes you plan to make will actually happen. It can be scary going from a place of safety to a place of the unknown. It's like moving from middle school to high school. There will be new people, a new schedule, and new things to learn and do.

But you can do it. Use your support system, follow up with the treatment plans you have established. Remember that you can be your own worst enemy or your own best friend.

No one can stop you from the things you plan to accomplish except for you. No one can keep you from being happy except you. I'm going to share this story with you and I want you to keep it in your heart when you are struggling. Know that you are just as strong as the person in this story. No, I take

that back. You are stronger!

The Story of Grace

Grace opened the cabinet carefully, ensuring it didn't fall off of its last hinge. A roach ran for cover and for some reason Grace wanted to go hide wherever that roach was planning to hide. That's how much she hated her life. She had been living in this raggedy apartment complex since she could remember. When she was old enough she just moved down the hall to her own apartment. This is the life she knew, section 8.

Growing up in the fast lane, she thought she knew all there was to know about life. But she fell in love with Kevin at 17 and then Deon 4 years later. She thought the love was true and that it would last forever. She was blinded by the reality of the relationships.

The men didn't want to go anywhere and they didn't plan on helping her get anywhere either. Both of them left her with a baby, a boy and a girl. Neither of the children had seen their fathers more than twice since their births.

But Grace did what she had to do. She worked part time at the super market during the week and worked as a cocktail waitress on the weekend. At least that was what she told her mom, who watched her children while she worked.

Her waitressing job actually turned into her being a private dancer. And also a drinker and a pothead.

Life was hard to deal with sober. Her bills still had to be paid and kept piling up. Her EBT card only stretched so far and often she had to let someone use it so she could get cash to pay other bills. She couldn't afford cable tv or the internet. That money was spent towards her car note, gas and electric bills. Anything left was spent at the thrift shop buying new clothes for the children.

She looked at her babies sitting over on the couch. A couch so used that the cushion being turned over could no longer hide the shabbiness. They were staring at one of the few free channels that came in. She never wanted or imagined this life for them.

Life had to get better. She didn't want her children to fall into the same cycle she did. Following the footsteps of her mom and her grandmother, surviving on section 8 and EBT, forgetting that hopes and dreams could ever be reality.

Grace wanted to do better. She needed to do better. But she didn't have more than a high school education and no money to start the business she so desired. She wanted to be an interior designer. She was very good at it despite the way her apartment looked. She couldn't afford the luxury of designing her place like she wanted to on her salary. Even still, she wouldn't waste such creativity on this shabby apartment.

These walls were closing in on her. She didn't know how long it would be before she totally lost it. Seeing the sad disappointed faces of her children when she had to fix them ramen noodles for dinner.......for the third night in a row.

They looked forward to going to school. She suspected only because they were guaranteed a good meal there and that the menu varied. She didn't want them to grow up with the same resentments she had towards her mom.

Money was becoming scarcer as the competition at her weekend job increased. She wasn't willing to do as many things as the other women which meant she didn't see as much money rolling in. Her mind was slowly leaning towards giving her children up for adoption. At least then they would have a better chance of growing up happy and successful. They wouldn't let the hood suck them in.

But she was going to continue to apply for the single mom programs they had. Many of the programs out there offered better housing, childcare, and a stipend so that single mothers could finish school. However, the competition was fierce.

So many were trying to come up out of the welfare way of life. Many of them required moving to another location. She didn't know if she was really ready for that.

Grace fixed the ramen noodles. With relief, her children sat down and ate silently. She sat on the couch and waited for them to finish. Once they were done, she bathed them and put them in their bed. A bed they would soon outgrow because the older they became, the less they could share the same space.

Grace went off to her room and took a quick cold shower. The water system wasn't that great but it was free so she didn't complain. She dried off then lay on her bed and lit one. She allowed her mind to begin fading as she smoked and smoked. Once she was high enough, she put it out in the ashtray.

As she did every night, sober, high, or slightly drunk, Grace prayed to God to give her the strength for tomorrow and to give her babies a better life. She closed her eyes and slept.

The alarm woke her the next morning. She rushed to get the children packed and dropped off at her mother's house so she could prepare for work. The same thought popped in her head as she dressed for work.

She hated her job. She spent five hours a day scanning, copying, and filing documents for a small law firm that barely paid over minimum wage. But something was better than nothing.

She hopped in her Honda and turned the ignition several times. Praying today wasn't the day it wouldn't start. She knew she needed a new ignition but with her budget they were very expensive, even a used one. She kept setting aside a few dollars here and there though for when she was forced to get one.

She sped down the interstate, listening to the morning show, shaking her head at the drama some people would advertise over the radio. Barely making it on time, she walked into the office and began working on the large stack of documents piled in her cubicle.

They needed all the documents scanned by Friday but it would be impossible at the rate that they kept adding documents. She went to her manager to let her know that she wouldn't be able to meet the deadline.

Her anger boiled over as her manager suggested she take a shorter lunch break or stay extended hours. However it would be without pay as overtime was not authorized. Grace's blood began to boil. She stood on her feet five hours a day and they expected her to cut her lunch and come in on her off time without pay? They had lost their minds.

Grace had had enough. She threw her badge on the desk and stormed out. Screw them and her job. She was done with this life. Everybody wanted and wanted and wanted and gave nothing in return. In those few moments of anger she had decided to go through with allowing her children to be adopted. She was done with this stress, living from check to check. They were better off with someone more stable.

She sped towards the adoption agency. She hesitated before she stepped out of the car. Her phone rang, momentarily distracting her. It was a bill collector. No, she didn't have the money. No, she didn't know when she would have it. And she didn't care what they put on her credit report or what actions they would take.

She hung up the phone and stormed into the agency. The receptionist asked how she could assist her. Grace requested information on giving children up for adoption. The woman gave her an information packet and documents to fill out if she decided to go through with her decision.

Grace got back in her raggedy car and drove. She drove blindly, not knowing where she was going. The emotions overwhelmed her yet nothing was coming out. They were consuming her and she felt she had no release.

There was nothing she could do any more. She had fought the good fight. She was physically and mentally exhausted.

She found herself turning into the pier parking lot. She left everything in her car. Purse, keys, and cell phone. She walked to the end of the quiet pier and stood on the edge. She couldn't swim. It would be easy to just throw herself in now.

Then she wouldn't have to face watching her children being taken away. She wouldn't have to live with the fact that she gave them up. Grace teetered on the brink of death.

In that moment, as she was about to take a step off, she heard footsteps and a soft cry. She turned to see a young woman on the edge of hopelessness as well.

"What do you have to cry about?" Grace asked the woman nastily. The woman had interrupted her courage to step over and it pissed her off. The woman had invaded her moment.

"Oh, it's nothing. Just my company." The young woman said. "I think I'm going to lose it."

Grace had no sympathy for the woman.

"You're crying because you MIGHT lose your company? Do you know how many people can say they even had their own company? How many people are presently unemployed?" Grace said incredulously.

"But it's like losing my dream," the lady whined. "I was supposed to be this superior interior decorator owning a well-known company. But the woman who worked for me backed out. She decided it wasn't for her."

Grace was astounded. Was God playing tricks on her? Was this a set-up? Would cameras pop out and scream "you've been fooled"?

"Well how much does the job pay?" Grace asked cautiously.

"It really depends on the job." The lady said as she began to calm down. She felt good about venting to this stranger. "Most jobs start at $1,000 and they can last from one week to a month".

"Keep talking." Grace said.

"Well the simple jobs such as hiring painters for a new paint job and ensuring they stay on task start at that price. That usually lasts a week. The jobs that require buying totally new furniture and redecorating everything usually runs from $5 to $10k. Those jobs typically last a month."

Grace's head begin to spin. This could not be real. Someone was messing with her.

"Well, I happen to know someone who has always had a knack for it. They don't have a degree in the field but they remain committed and is definitely looking for coaching in the area. She's actually searching for a job too so maybe you can help each other out."

The woman was desperate. "Can you call her? Can you call her now? I need her right away. She can be my assistance until she is ready to take jobs on her own." The lady gushed out. This was fate. Her business would be saved. She wouldn't have to stand up the customers whose jobs she already accepted. She would have help.

Grace smiled. "Well, I won't be able to call her."

The woman's face began to sadden. "Why not?"

Grace smiled and thanked God.

"Because you're talking to her right now."

Discussion

- What opportunities would Grace have missed if she had stepped off of the pier? (Consider family, friends, children, job opportunities)

- Do you want to accidentally miss your opportunity? If not, then what must you do?

Epilogue

Cheyenne

My officer in charge picked me up from the rehabilitation center. I was silent on the way back as she told me how everyone was gearing up for deployment. Everyone was mostly in training at another camp. I wouldn't be going but my enlisted superior had a special temporary duty for me. I would travel the United States with other active duty members for 3 months, telling various organizations about my military experiences.

I was exhausted and not ready to face my unit anyway. All I wanted to do was settle back into my room and relax. I needed my life to be normal. And I intended to do it without the alcohol. They dropped me off in the front of my building and I headed up to my room. I came back out to smoke and looked across the parking lot. I saw Trishton's car. Old habits die really hard. I opened my phone and I dialed his number……..

Jennifer

This was my second chance. I still hadn't heard from my family after the letter I wrote to them. Although that hurt a little, I wouldn't let the pain consume me. I could be "normal". I was headed to a half-way house with women who understood where I was coming from and where I was headed.

The bus pulled into the station and I rushed to get inside the terminal. It reeked of stale cigarettes and urine but it provided heat against the chill that lingered outside. I was anxious to settle in. There were so many things I wanted to do to get my life back on track. I needed to find a job so I could have an honest income. I wanted to complete my high school diploma. Finally, I wanted to live happily.

My house mother, Loretta, greeted me near the front door of the bus terminal with a firm but friendly smile. We embraced in a very strong hug. A hug that said "I'm here for you". I looked over her shoulder and I tensed up. My thoughts of that fearful moment had just became my reality. Dre was standing over in the corner………..watching me…..

119

Ashley

I didn't feel a sense of relief like the other women did. I was nervous. Nervous about returning to my unit. Even if it was just to give my testimony and to pack my things. They decided that they would move me to another unit until my case was closed. Once it was over they would allow me to change duty stations and start brand new. But until then I would need to deal with the whispers, the stares, the accusing eyes.

The plane ride didn't seem long enough. I wanted to stay up in the clouds forever. Never come back down to earth. I learned some useful techniques in rehab. From relaxation, to communication, to coping with stress in positive ways. But that last weekend, when they gave us a day to go out in town as group therapy, no one knew I had made a significant purchase. It was a purchase that would change my life.

I grabbed my carry-on bag and proceeded to baggage claims. Once I had my luggage, I went outside where the command driver was waiting for me. We made our way back to base in silence. So much to do, so many things will be different now. A tear trickled down my face as I looked in my purse. And stared at the reality of a positive pregnancy test………

Tasha

I was floating on cloud 8, not quite on cloud 9. I'm reserving cloud nine for when I've achieved all of my goals. I was ready to deal with life and all of its struggles once again. I was decked out in my Beyoncé wig, a mixture of brown and blonde flowing down my back. I had my stilettos back on. Looking great in my skinny jeans and off the shoulder sweater.

I missed my apartment. The luxury, the comfort, the peace. I still had to check in with my parole officer every month but I was ready. No more prison time for me which meant no more smoking. I had to accept me and accept the world as is. I needed to find a job, get into things I liked like make-up, fashion designing, or modeling. I was ready to get my life right so that I could find my Mr. Right.

I approached my door and saw a beautiful bouquet of flowers that seemed like they had been there for at least a day. They were weathered but the beauty was not gone. I picked them up and took them inside. I threw my bags by the door and placed the flowers on my counter. My house smelled like no one had been in it for a while. Cleaning. Another thing on my to do list. Curiosity took over. I sat on a bar stool and opened the card that came with the flowers.

"Sorry cannot express the way I feel. It could never make up for the things that have happened or the time you lost by being in prison. But if it takes the rest of my life to make it up to you, I will. I was afraid. Afraid to admit that regardless of the fact that you kept your secret from me, I had truly fallen in love with you. I don't care who you are, man or woman. But I am willing to accept who I am and who you are. I love you. Let me show you truly how much."

It was the man. The man I went to prison for. The man who I loved but who also rejected me. I picked up the vase, threw it across the room, and watched it shatter into pieces…………

Lorie

My parents had kept in contact with me since I was in rehab. I received a letter every so often letting me know they were thinking of me. Well not necessarily thinking of me. I believe they were more worried about their image. They were hoping this would change my life before it was too late. They had sent me a new house key. I guess it was their way of welcoming me back home. Wait, let me not assume they have their own personal intentions. Maybe they do truly care about me and realize that they have neglected me.

I was excited as the plane landed. The grass looked greener than I ever remembered. Maybe because this was my first time being clean in a while. I would be able to enjoy life again. There would be many things that I would still need to change, that I would need to openly express to my family. But now I felt a greater sense of patience, of peace. A greater belief in my ability to communicate to them properly and firmly.

The chauffeur picked me up and I enjoyed the ride home in luxury. I didn't appreciate the life I had nearly enough.

I grabbed a bottle of water from the mini fridge and sunk lower into the plush seats. Pedestrians gawked at the car. Homeless men and women glared. The scenery changed from mediocre to grand as we entered my parents' upscale neighborhood.

Blue lights flashed in the front yard as we pulled up. Neighbors were on the sidewalk, gawking. Trying to get a better view of what was going on. My heart sped up in a panic. I slowly got out of the car. That's when I saw my brother, Christian. Tears streamed down his face. I rushed up to him. In broken words, he said "*they're dead, place trashed, dead...*".

My world started fading. One thought popped into my head before I blacked out. I would never be able to show my parents who I could truly be...................

Stay Tuned.....

If you thoroughly enjoyed learning about these women as they went through rehabilitation then you'll have a chance to see what their lives were like before rehab and afterwards.

Each angel will have her own book before and after rehab, going through the life she experienced and seeing the changes she made and who she became.

Amazingly, Cheyenne will wow you as her story is based on the life story of the author.

Go to **www.discoveredangel.com**:

- To share or read inspirational stories
- Order books, check the dates for new book coming soon
- Set up the author as an inspirational speaker
- Order journals and other accessories to help you through you journey

Also on **Facebook** and **Twitter** as Discovered Angel.

Coming Soon.......

Going back two years before Cheyenne went to
rehabilitation....

The Lost Angel: Cheyenne

June 15, 2005

Dumb, dumb, Shy

What the hell was that about today? I've been pestering
Trishton about loving me and being with me and he hasn't
budged. Even my classmate, that nosey little soldier, said that he
was telling everyone else he was single. Lo and behold I
confronted him and pissed him off.

Trishton might be half crazy though. I probably
shouldn't have blasted that man hating music in the car on the
way back from the river walk. But I just didn't know how to
express myself. And when he turned the music off completely, I
got pissed.

Stopped the car in the middle of the road, got out, and
started walking. Where the hell was I going anyway? Base was a

127

long walk away. But Trishton parked and came right after me.

For a brief second I felt truly loved because many men wouldn't

come after a woman but he did........